Robert La Salle

Discover The Life Of An Explorer

Trish Kline

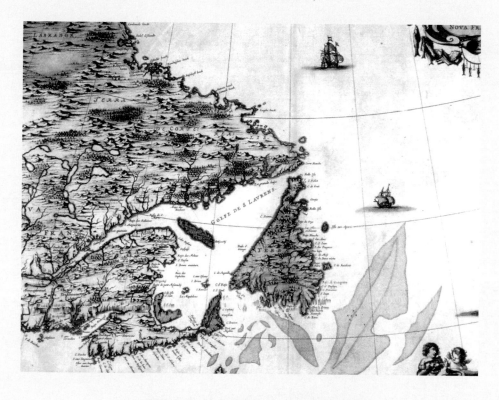

Rourke Publishing LLC
Vero Beach, Florida 32964

PHOTO CREDITS:
©Getty Images: cover, page 18; ©Canadian Heritage, National Archives of
Canada: Title page, pages 7, 12, 17; ©Culver Pictures: pages 4, 10, 21;
©James P. Rowan: page 9; ©Artville LLC: page 13; Library of Congress: page 15

EDITORIAL SERVICES:
Pamela Schroeder

Library of Congress Cataloging-in-Publication Data

Kline, Trish.
    Robert La Salle / Trish Kline.
        p. cm. — (Discover the life of an explorer)
    Includes bibliographical references (p.) and index.
    ISBN 1-58952-069-6
    1. La Salle, Robert Cavelier, sieur de, 1643-1687—Juvenile literature. 2.
Explorers—North America—Biography—Juvenile literature. 3. Explorers—
France—Biography—Juvenile literature. 4. North America—Discovery and
exploration—French—Juvenile literature. 5. Mississippi River Valley—
Discovery and exploration—French—Juvenile literature. 6. Canada—
History—To 1763 (New France)—Juvenile literature. [1. La Salle, Robert
Cavelier, sieur de, 1643-1687. 2. Explorers. 3. Mississippi River—Discovery
and exploration.] I. Title

    F1030.5 .k5 2001
    977'.01'092—dc21
    [B]   2001018590

Printed in the USA

TABLE OF CONTENTS

BEFORE THE ADVENTURE BEGAN

Robert La Salle was born in 1643. He lived in France. When he was young, he wanted to be a **priest**. He lived with the priests. They taught him to read and write. After nine years, La Salle decided he would not become a priest. He wanted to have great adventures.

La Salle wanted to be an explorer.

ARRIVING IN THE NEW WORLD

In 1666 La Salle sailed for the country of Canada. He was going to be a trader. He traded with the Native Americans. He gave them cloth and other goods for furs. La Salle explored the area near his trading post. He got to know the **language** and ways of the Native Americans. Because of these skills, he was made the **commander** of a fort. This fort was called Fort Frontenac.

La Salle was the commander of Fort Frontenac.

FORTS AND TRADING POSTS

In 1677, La Salle visited the king of France. He asked the king for money to explore new areas of the New World. He told the king that he would build forts and trading posts. In 1680 La Salle began to explore the upper Mississippi River.

La Salle explored the upper Mississippi in 1680.

EXPLORING THE RIVER

In 1682 La Salle explored the Mississippi River all the way to the Gulf of Mexico. La Salle claimed all the land along the Mississippi River for France. He named the area Louisiana for King Louis XIV, king of France. He built many forts in Louisiana.

Fort St. Louis was built by
La Salle and his men.

The Griffon, built by La Salle, was used to carry trade goods.

La Salle searched for the mouth of the Mississippi in the Gulf of Mexico.

A VERY HAPPY KING

In 1683 La Salle returned to France. The king was very happy about all of the land La Salle had claimed for France. He decided that La Salle should build **colonies**. La Salle would **govern** the new colonies. The colonies were built from Lake Michigan to the Gulf of Mexico.

La Salle claimed land for King Louis XIV.

The king also gave La Salle four ships, supplies, and men. He wanted La Salle to sail to the Gulf of Mexico. Then he wanted La Salle to build a colony at the mouth of the Mississippi River.

The king told La Salle to build a colony at the mouth of the Mississippi.

A FAILED MISSION

La Salle sailed to the Gulf of Mexico. But he could not find the Mississippi River. He became lost and landed on the shore of present-day Texas. He was many miles from the Mississippi River. He tried to cross the land to the river, but he failed.

La Salle's men grew tired and angry. They turned against him and killed him. La Salle died in 1687 near a river in Texas. He was 44 years old.

La Salle's men turned against him and killed him.

SUCCESS REMEMBERED

Though he did not find the mouth of the Mississippi River from the sea, La Salle had many successes. He was the first to explore the whole Mississippi River. He claimed a large part of the New World for France. He is remembered as one of the great **explorers** of North America.

La Salle claimed the Louisiana Territory for France.

IMPORTANT DATES TO REMEMBER

1643	Born in France.
1666	Sailed to Canada.
1677	Returned to France to ask for money for more exploration
1682	Explored the Mississippi River region to the Gulf of Mexico.
1683	Prepared for a voyage to the Gulf of Mexico and the mouth of the Mississippi.
1685	Landed on the Texas gulf coast.
1687	Died in Texas (March 20).

GLOSSARY

colonies (KAHL eh neez) — places in a country where people live but are ruled by another country

commander (ke MAN der) — the person in charge

explorers (ik SPLOR erz) — people who travel to unknown places

govern (GUV ern) — to rule

language (LANG gwij) — words spoken by a tribe or other related group of people

priest (PREEST) — a religious title; a person who serves the church

INDEX

Further Reading

Jacobs, William Jay. *LaSalle: A Life of Boundless Adventure*. Franklin Watts, 1994.
Coulter, Tony. *LaSalle and the Explorers of the Mississippi*. Chelsea House, 1991.

Websites To Visit

www.encarta.msn.com
www.gale.com

About The Author

Trish Kline is a seasoned curriculum writer. She has written a great number of nonfiction books for the school and library market. Her print publishing credits include two dozen books as well as hundreds of newspaper and magazine articles, anthologies, short stories, poetry, and plays. She currently resides in Helena, Montana.

jB
LASALLE

Kline, Trish.

Robert La Salle.

$18.60

DATE			